King Arthur

New and future titles in the series include:

The Mystery Library

King Arthur

Michael J. Wyly

Lucent Books, Inc.
P.O. Box 289011, San Diego, California

On Cover: Duncan's *The Taking of Excalibur*

Library of Congress Cataloging-in-Publication Data

Wyly, Michael J., 1970–
  King Arthur / by Michael J. Wyly.
    p. cm.—(The mystery library)
Includes bibliographical references (p.) and index.
Summary: A comprehensive look at the evolution of the
Arthurian legend. Investigates the probable identity of the real
5th century Arthur so as to uncover the process by which the
fable developed over the centuries.
  ISBN 1-56006-771-3 (hardback : alk. paper)
  1. Arthur, King—Juvenile literature. 2. Britons—Kings and
rulers—Juvenile literature. 3. Great Britain—Antiquities,
Celtic—Juvenile literature. 4. Great Britain—History—To
1066—Juvenile literature. 5. Arthurian romances—Sources—
Juvenile literature. [1. Arthur, King. 2. Kings, queens, rulers, etc.
3. Great Britain—History—To 1066.]
I. Title. II. Mystery library (Lucent Books)
  DA152.5.A7 W94 2001
  942.01 4—dc21

                    2001000855

Copyright 2001 by Lucent Books, Inc.
P.O. Box 289011, San Diego, California 92198-9011

Printed in the U.S.A.

Contents

Foreword

In Shakespeare's immortal play, *Hamlet*, the young Danish aristocrat Horatio has clearly been astonished and disconcerted by his encounter with a ghost-like apparition on the castle battlements. "There are more things in heaven and earth," his friend Hamlet assures him, "than are dreamt of in your philosophy."

Many people today would readily agree with Hamlet that the world and the vast universe surrounding it are teeming with wonders and oddities that remain largely outside the realm of present human knowledge or understanding. How did the universe begin? What caused the dinosaurs to become extinct? Was the lost continent of Atlantis a real place or merely legendary? Does a monstrous creature lurk beneath the surface of Scotland's Loch Ness? These are only a few of the intriguing questions that remain unanswered, despite the many great strides made by science in recent centuries.

Lucent Books' Mystery Library series is dedicated to exploring these and other perplexing, sometimes bizarre, and often disturbing or frightening wonders. Each volume in the series presents the best-known tales, incidents, and evidence surrounding the topic in question. Also included are the opinions and theories of scientists and other experts who have attempted to unravel and solve the ongoing mystery. And supplementing this information is a fulsome list of sources for further reading, providing the reader with the means to pursue the topic further.

The Mystery Library will satisfy every young reader's fascination for the unexplained. As one of history's greatest scientists, physicist Albert Einstein, put it:

The most beautiful thing we can experience is the mysterious. It is the source of all true art and science. He to whom this emotion is a stranger, who can no longer wonder and stand rapt in awe, is as good as dead: his eyes are closed.

Lost in Legend

There is a legend that says that on the eve of the Dark Ages of ancient Britain, a starlike object appeared in the sky that could be seen both by day and by night. Proceeding from the star was a single ray of light. At the end of the light was the fiery shape of a dragon, and from the dragon's mouth there were two other beams of light, one of which stretched across Gaul to the south. The other reached west toward the Irish Sea only to split again into seven smaller shafts of light.

Merlin—an ancient, wise wizard who was the son of a mortal woman and her demon lover—gazed upon this star and made a prophecy. The star and the dragon, Merlin stated, represent Uther, the next king of Britain. Uther will battle the enemy until the coming of his son, Arthur. The beam of light that stretches to the south symbolizes Arthur, Merlin continued, and Arthur will unite and rule all of the lands covered by the beam. The second beam signifies Arthur's own sons and daughters who will follow him to rule the kingdom of Britain. With this pronouncement, Merlin foretold the coming of one of history's greatest legends, that of King Arthur.

The legend of King Arthur arose during the Dark Ages of fifth-century Britain when horrendous wars and hordes of invading barbarians threatened the people of the ancient island—descendants of Celtic tribes and their Roman conquerors—who called themselves Britons. Their lives were in shambles; their farms and houses were looted and burned; and their leadership was too weak and powerless to stop the pillaging Saxons from the south.

There is a slim volume of historical evidence, however, that suggests that the ancient Britons experienced a revival that began around A.D. 480 or 500 and lasted about forty years. This era is called the Golden Age of Britain because

A statue depicts King Arthur, one of the world's most famous legendary heroes.

Proving the existence of King Arthur and his knights has been difficult because the legend has been rewritten over the centuries.

the Britons managed to reunify themselves under a central leader, most likely a king. Under this leadership, the Britons halted the murderous campaigns of the barbarians and established a prosperous and peaceful society.

Do these historical events indicate that Arthur, the fabled king of legend, did indeed exist? Could this heroic figure actually have led his people to the Golden Age so often described in legend? These questions lie at the heart of the mystery surrounding King Arthur.

Proving Arthur's existence has been difficult. Few historical documents from this period have survived. Much of what is known of Arthur, his kingdom, his knights, and the Round Table comes from the legends themselves. But these stories of King Arthur have been rewritten and enhanced over the centuries. All actual facts seem to have been lost or hidden. As a result, the search for King Arthur has proven to be one of the greatest historical mysteries of our time. And to begin the mysterious journey, we must go to the legendary tales written by a true-to-life Middle Age knight, Sir Thomas Malory.

Chapter 1

From Boy to King

The legend of King Arthur has been an important part of the history of England since before the Early Middle Ages. However, before the fifteenth century, approximately one thousand years after Arthur is said to have governed England from his throne at Camelot, there had been very few efforts to collect all of the tales of Arthur's legendary exploits into a single volume. And there were none whatsoever in the English language. However, in 1485, Sir Thomas Malory's book *Le Morte D'Arthur (The Death of Arthur)* was published under the commission of King Henry VII.

Malory's book was an English translation of the French versions of the Arthurian legend. In fact, *Morte D'Arthur* is one of the most important English sources for understanding the legend of King Arthur. However, in collecting the Arthurian tales into a single volume in English, Malory also included references to his own time and culture. Malory's version of the legend is therefore a mix of the Arthurian legends of fifth-century Britain and references to fifteenth-century social and political life. One of the difficulties of deciphering the legend is understanding how and why Malory added these references. The investigation into the mystery of King Arthur begins with an understanding of fifteenth-century England.

The Revival of Arthur

In the fifteenth century, England's interest in King Arthur had to do with the origin of the word *Britain*. Almost one thousand years before, during the fifth century, the island of England had been inhabited by groups of warriors and their families who called themselves Britons. According to legend, King Arthur rose from among them and united the warring factions, unifying England as a country. Under Arthur's leadership, the Britons created a mighty kingdom.

In 1485, the English aristocracy was again working to unify England. England was at war with itself as two powerful families, the Houses of York and Lancaster, fought for control of the country. This civil war, called the War of

Disunity and strife prevailed in England as Richard III (pictured) sought to secure the English throne for himself.

13

the Roses, occurred because the houses of both York and Lancaster disagreed about which house should control the English throne. Two wars had already been fought over this issue since 1455. The third and final war began in 1483 when King Edward IV of the House of Lancaster died. Richard III of York assumed the throne, but only by murdering the rightful heirs, the sons of Edward IV. The third war occurred as a result of these murders. In 1485, the leader of the House of Lancaster, Henry Tudor, defeated the murderous Richard III and became Henry VII, the new king of England. But the war between the Houses of York and Lancaster continued for another two years.

Because Henry was anxious to end the war and gain acceptance of his kingship from the English people, he began to claim that he was a descendant of King Arthur. He wanted to share the legend of Arthur with his allies and his opponents because he felt that it would help solidify his rule. But there was a problem: Not one complete record of Arthur's legend existed in English because the English language had only recently replaced French as the language of the English courts.

To ensure that a complete version of the King Arthur legend was available in English, Henry VII ordered his court translator and publisher, William Caxton, to publish the stories of the knight and writer Sir Thomas Malory. Malory had already written his accounts of Arthur several years before and was anxious to publish a complete English version that reflected well on the English nobility and set an example for the English people. Most of Malory's sources were from the French. Like most English aristocracy, Malory had a strong foundation in the French language and was also very well versed in the French tales of King Arthur and his knights. Furthermore, Malory possessed a greater skill of the English language than his fellow writers in Britain did.

Wanting to prove that he was the rightful heir to the English throne, King Henry VII claimed he was a descendant of King Arthur.

Malory's collection of Arthur's legendary exploits was published later that same year under the title *Le Morte D'Arthur.* The title was given to the collection by Caxton, not by Malory; it alludes to the heroic last battle in which Arthur was mortally wounded. Malory's text not only became the most popular Arthurian text of his times but continues to dominate what is known of the Arthurian legend today.

Malory's Legend

Although Malory's story was adapted from French and Latin sources, Malory also elaborated on the story himself. He incorporated issues, rules, and customs of his own time within the Arthurian stories so that the myth of Arthur was more appealing and more relevant to his readers.

Pictured is a replica of a page from Sir Thomas Malory's Le Morte D'Arthur.

¶Here foloweth the fyrth boke of the noble and worthy prynce kyng Arthur.

¶How syr Launcelot and syr Lyonell departed fro the courte for to seke aduentures / & how syr Lyonell lefte syr Launcelot slepynge & was taken. Capitulo.j.

None after that the noble & worthy kyng Arthur was comen fro Rome into Englande / all the knyghtes of the rounde table resorted vnto þ kyng and made many iustes and turneymentes / & some there were that were good knyghtes / whiche encreased so in armes and worshyp that they passed all theyr felowes in prowesse & noble dedes & that was well proued on many. But in especyall it was proued on syr Launcelot du lake. for in all turneymentes and iustes and dedes of armes / bothe for lyfe and deth he passed all knyghtes & at no tyme he was neuer ouercomen but yf it were by treason or enchauntement. Syr Launcelot encreased so meruaylously in worshyp & honour / wherfore he is the first knyght þ the frensshe booke maketh mencyon of / after that kynge Arthur came from Rome / wherfore quene Gueneuer had hym in grete fauour aboue all other knyghtes / and certaynly he loued the quene agayne aboue all other ladyes and damoyselles all the dayes of his lyfe / and for her he

i ii

Despite the obvious fiction in *Morte D'Arthur*, Malory's work was still treated as a historical text. Much of this had to do with the medieval mind-set toward history, which varies greatly from that today. As Geoffrey Ashe explains,

> Medieval ideas about authenticity were unlike our own. A modern historical novelist is frankly writing fiction, yet even so, such a novelist will try to get the period right: to find out how the characters would have lived, how they would have dressed, what they would have eaten, what their interests and customs would have been. In the Middle Ages, authors did not do this, since authenticity did not matter to them in the same way. When they handled an ancient story, they medievalized it, making the characters very much like their own contemporaries.[1]

Malory's book was further reinforced as a historical text by Caxton's introduction to the work in which he praises *Morte D'Arthur* as a historically relevant document.

The importance of history to the English should not be underestimated. For the English of the fifteenth century, the stories of King Arthur were not only a source of romantic heroism but also a record of an English king who united England. It excited the English to think that Arthur established a glorious society. Thus, it is not surprising that Malory's story enjoyed instant popularity, for he gave his people tales of an English king who had fought to create their country.

For the fifteenth-century English, the most important Arthurian tales were those that showed Arthur's rise to kingship because they justified the right of King Henry VII and his kin to control their country. In Britain, a king must be of noble blood in order to rule. Because Christianity and politics were deeply enmeshed, the

English of the Middle Ages believed that only those of royal descent had been given by God the right to rule over the country. Malory's version of the Arthurian legends mirrored this system of beliefs. Thus, it was important that Malory explain Arthur's lineage to assure his medieval readership of Arthur's legitimate claim to the throne. In other words, Malory needed to demonstrate that Arthur, despite the fact that his father gained the throne through war, was the rightful heir to the throne. Likewise, this also established the legitimacy of King Henry VII, who also took the throne in war. Malory begins *Morte D'Arthur* by explaining who Arthur's father was and then detailing the chain of events that led to Arthur's birth.

The Legendary Birth of Arthur

In Malory's *Morte D'Arthur,* the nobility of pre-Arthurian Britain were also in a state of civil war. Noblemen fought noblemen in an effort to gain control of more land and power. The two primary rivals were both men of noble and powerful houses. One was the duke of Tintagel. The other was Arthur's future father, King Uther Pendragon. Unlike the duke, King Uther was a descendant of the previous kings of England. Furthermore, while the duke was more interested in war than peace, King Uther sought to unify the land of England and create a prosperous nation. After much fighting, King Uther was on the verge of success, and the duke agreed to a truce. More important, he agreed to pledge himself to Uther's kingship.

Unfortunately for Uther, his efforts to unite his kingdom were spoiled by his own jealousy and lust. On the night of a great feast to celebrate the newly formed peace, Uther fell in love with the duke of Tintagel's wife, Igraine. Angry with Uther's advances toward his wife, the duke withdrew from Uther's palace. In order to win Igraine from the duke, Uther summoned his forces and attacked the duke's castle, called Terrabil. The war raged and many knights died on both sides, but neither the duke nor King Uther could claim victory. They were at a standstill. The appearance of Merlin eventually turned the tides for Uther.

According to legend, Merlin was a magician who sought to protect the English throne from any but the rightful king. In the midst of the battle at Terrabil, Merlin appeared at

According to legend, the magician Merlin helped King Uther defeat his enemies in exchange for Uther's firstborn son, Arthur.

Uther's side and offered aid. But there was a price for his help. Merlin demanded that Uther give him his first-born son so that he could protect him until it was time for his boy, to be named Arthur, to take the throne. Uther agreed:

> Sir, said Merlin, I know all your heart every deal; so ye will be sworn unto me as ye be a true king anointed, to fulfill my desire, ye shall have your desire. Then the king was sworn upon the four Evangelists. Sir, said Merlin, this is my desire: the first night that you shall lie by Igraine ye shall get a child on her, and when that is born, that it shall be delivered to me for to nourish there as I will have it; for it shall be your worship, and the child's avail as mickle [much] as the child is worth. I will well, said the king, as thou wilt have it.[2]

With the aid of Merlin's magic, Uther defeated and killed the duke and claimed Igraine as his prize.

When Arthur was born, Merlin again appeared, this time at the gates of Uther's own castle, and the king sent his newborn son to him. Merlin took the baby Arthur and entrusted his care to an honorable knight, Sir Ector, who raised him as his adopted son. As Malory writes,

> The king commanded two knights and two ladies to take the child, bound in a cloth of gold, and that ye deliver him to what poor man ye meet at the postern gate of the castle. So the child was delivered unto Merlin, and so he bare forth unto Sir Ector, and made an holy man to christen him, and named him Arthur.[3]

Despite King Uther Pendragon's victory at Terrabil and his winning of Arthur's mother, Igraine, he lost the trust of the surrounding nobility. These problems were combined with the foreign hordes from the north who had begun to raid Uther's lands as a result of the weakened condition of

his forces, the result of his losses at Terrabil. In addition, King Uther himself fell gravely ill. However, he had one last legendary moment of glory. With Merlin by his side, King Uther fought a final great battle, driving the enemies of England back to the north. According to legend, three days after his return to his castle, Uther died.

Merlin arranged for a great tournament of knights in order to select a new king and bring about peace.

The Land Without a King

With the death of King Uther, the land of the Britons experienced even more conflict. Merlin kept Arthur's location and existence a secret. Without an heir to the throne, the nobility increased their struggles for power and control. Some took sides against others. Alliances were formed and lost. All hope for a unified England disappeared under the possibility of an intense and lengthy civil war.

As strife mounted amid the controversy over the throne of England, there were increasing calls for peace. In hopes of achieving a peace, Merlin arranged for a great tournament of knights to commence New Year's Day. According to Malory's version of the legend, knights from all over England were invited to prove their courage and physical strength through the art of sword and lance. Knights charged each other on horseback with blunted lances and participated in a number of contests, including mock duels and races, designed to test their ability with a sword and a horse. The Britons hoped that the winner of the tournament would prove himself worthy of occupying the British throne. At last, peace tentatively reigned.

A Miraculous Discovery

Although Merlin knew that Arthur was the rightful heir to the throne, he still had to prove his right to claim the Crown to the nobility. On the day before the tournament, Arthur's right to claim the English Crown was confirmed by a miracle. Among the knights at the tournament was Sir Ector, who brought with him his eldest son Sir Kay and Kay's adopted brother and squire, the unsuspecting Arthur. On the day before the tournament, while all the guests were attending a mass, a sword driven through both an iron anvil and a stone slab appeared in the churchyard. On the sword was an inscription. According to Malory,

> There was seen in the churchyard, against the high altar, a great stone four square, like unto a marble stone; and in the midst thereof was like an anvil of steel a foot on high, and therein stuck a fair sword naked by the point, and letters there were written in gold about the sword that said thus:—Whoso pulleth out this sword of this stone and anvil, is rightwise king born of all England.[4]

Many great lords attempted to pull the sword from the stone, but none succeeded. The plan to hold a tournament continued. On the next day, all of the knights assembled in the field for their mock battles, among them Sir Kay and his squire, Arthur.

As a squire, Arthur's duties were to care for Kay's weapons, armor, and horse. The legend states that Kay's sword had been left behind at his father's home. It was therefore Arthur's obligation, as Kay's squire, to retrieve the sword so that Kay could participate in the tournament. Unable to locate Kay's sword and desperate to aid his brother and fulfill his duty as a squire, Arthur went to the churchyard to retrieve the sword in the stone that had so miraculously appeared. Arthur approached the anvil and stone and, with a single pull, released the sword. Malory writes,

Then was Arthur wroth, and said to himself, I will ride to the churchyard, and take the sword with me

IVRE REX BRITANNIÆ

This illustration shows Arthur as he pulls the sword from the stone.

that sticketh in the stone, for my brother Sir Kay shall not be without a sword this day. So when he came to the churchyard, Sir Arthur alit and ties his horse to the stile. . . . And so he handled the sword by the handles, and lightly and fiercely pulled it out of the stone.[5]

Not understanding the impact of what he had accomplished, Arthur hastened to Kay's side to give the sword to him. When Sir Kay and the other knights realized the origin of the sword and that Arthur had pulled it from the stone, they all kneeled to him. Confused, the young Arthur turned to his adopted father, who explained to him the truth of the young king's origins, that Merlin had delivered Arthur to Ector in order to hide him and that he was meant to be king. Malory's version of the legend says that a coronation soon followed in which Arthur was formally crowned king of the Britons.

Historically, however, Malory's version of the tournament cannot possibly be accurate. Malory incorporated his fifteenth-century lifestyle into his adaptation of the Arthurian legend, for it was not until the Late Middle Ages that the tournament became an accepted form of sport, and it was during Malory's time, not Arthur's, that knights routinely took part in tournaments to prove their noble and virtuous qualities. Malory's additions to the story allowed his English audience to connect the life of King Arthur to their own lives. He ensured that they would understand and enjoy his story.

Queen Guinevere

The tale of King Arthur's queen, Guinevere (known as Guenever in Malory's book) is another example of how Malory used the tales of King Arthur to mirror the society of fifteenth-century England. Although Malory did not invent the character of Queen Guinevere, Malory's audi-

Malory may have included the character of Guinevere in Le Morte D'Arthur *to remind Henry VII of his responsibility to marry someone of royal blood.*

ence expected him to include her because it was important to show that Arthur married a woman of royal blood. In the fifteenth century, it was the king's responsibility to marry a woman of royal birth in order to have children that could take his place once he died. Should a king fail to live up to this responsibility, others who desired the power of

25

kingship might try to take the throne for themselves after the king's death. According to legend, Arthur and Guinevere did not have any children, and this was one of the reasons the Golden Age came to an end. Similarly, Malory's England did not have a clear heir to the throne. With the inclusion of Guinevere, Malory sought to remind King Henry VII of his kingly responsibilities.

The tale of Guinevere, Arthur's future queen, is one fraught with potential tragedy from the beginning. It begins when Merlin confronts Arthur with his wisdom and magic by reading a dark future for Arthur and his wife-to-

This engraving by Gustave Dore shows King Arthur as he sends Guinevere away after she betrays him.

be. In *Morte D'Arthur*, Arthur turns to Merlin for advice after his most trusted allies insist that he marry in order to maintain the royal line. Malory writes,

> So it fell on a time King Arthur said to Merlin, My barons will let me have no rest, but needs I must take a wife, and I will none take but thy counsel and by thine advice. It is well done, said Merlin, that ye take a wife, for a man of your bounty and noblesse should not be without a wife. Now is there any that ye love more than another? Yea, said King Arthur, I love Guenever the king's daughter, Leodegrance of the land of Cameliard, that which holdeth in his house the Table Round that ye told he had of my father Uther. And this damosel is the most valiant and fairest lady that I know living, or yet that ever I could find.[6]

However, in his choice of Lady Guinevere, King Arthur incurs a warning from his adviser, Merlin:

> Sir, said Merlin, as of her beauty and fairness she is one of the fairest on live, but, an ye loved her not so well as ye do, I should find you a damosel of beauty and of goodness that should like you and please you, an your heart were not set; but there as a man's heart is set, he will be loth to return. That is truth, said King Arthur. But Merlin warned the king covertly that Guenever was not wholesome for him to take to wife, for he warned him that Launcelot should love her, and she him again.[7]

Merlin rightly predicts that Guinevere will betray Arthur when she falls in love with Arthur's best knight and most trusted ally, Lancelot.

Despite Merlin's warnings, Arthur chooses Guinevere as his wife. According to the legend, when Guinevere arrives at Camelot, it is with one hundred knights carrying

Arthur's conflict with Lancelot eventually leads to his death at the hands of Mordred (pictured).

the ancestral table of Arthur's father, the Round Table. These knights, along with those already under Arthur's command, defended Arthur's England until his final days. During that time, the knights went on quests and adventures in their efforts to maintain their duty to king and country. Some of these knights performed perhaps the most famous of Arthurian tales, the Quest for the Holy Grail (a cup associated with miraculous powers of healing and sustenance).

Much later in the Arthurian epic, Merlin's prophecies regarding Guinevere come true, and Arthur is forced to send Guinevere away without producing an heir. This event also pushed him to war with Lancelot and gives a new challenger, Mordred, an opportunity to steal his throne. In fact, Arthur's death results from his having to wage war on Mordred; both Arthur and Mordred were killed as a result. Of even more importance to Malory, however, was the absence of children between Guinevere and Arthur. No children meant that no new king could assume the throne, causing the Golden Age to come to an end. This was an error that Malory did not want to see repeated by Henry VII. Malory used the Arthurian legend to remind his king that he must produce legitimate heirs to safeguard the throne.

The Unification of England

With Arthur's ascension to the throne, the kingdom of England unified and secured from harm, and King Arthur's marriage to a lady of noble birth, the first cycle of Malory's telling of the Arthurian legend is complete. Yet the story raises many questions. *Morte D'Arthur* is a mix of so many fictions that it becomes difficult to believe that a figure such as King Arthur could have actually existed. Was there really a king that unified England during the so-called Dark Ages? Did he possess the military prowess attributed to the legendary Arthur? Did he indeed command a body of knights who pronounced judgments at a

Historians, scholars, and archaeologists continue to search for answers about the King Arthur legend.

round table? Or is the Arthurian epic simply a made-up tale maintained to justify King Henry VII's claim to the throne? These are questions that have been asked by a great number of historians, scholars, and archaeologists, each of whom has engaged on a quest of their own: to find the real Arthur.

Chapter 2

Who Was the Real Arthur?

If King Arthur really existed, he would have lived in the late fifth century during England's Dark Ages, before written historical records were regularly made and kept. During the Dark Ages, the British Isles were constantly threatened by warring factions of barbarians. Arthur is said to have emerged from the chaos of these wars and unified Britain, achieving a time of peace and prosperity for his people.

Although we know that the romanticized legend of Arthur, as put forth by Sir Thomas Malory, is mostly fiction, historians have still asked whether or not there is some truth behind the myth. Despite the obvious impossibilities of the Arthurian saga, by Malory's time, tales of Arthur had survived for almost one thousand years. Furthermore, there are a number of facts that historians and archaeologists have uncovered that lead them to conclude that a real Arthur probably did exist.

More and more, the real mystery centers around answering the question who was the real Arthur? To find out, it is first necessary to explore the true state of affairs within the so-called Dark Ages of Britain in order to understand the world and the country in which the real Arthur would have lived.

Unsteady Rome

For five hundred years, the Isle of Britain and its Celtic people were under the control of the Roman Empire. However, on August 24, A.D. 410, what for centuries had seemed impossible occurred: Rome was looted by the Goths, an invading army of barbarians. Even though Rome

The sack of Rome in A.D. 410 weakened Roman power in the British Isles.

made a brief recovery, the first signs of a troubled Roman Empire—which was the center of power and civilization for much of western Europe and Britain—were becoming apparent.

The looting of Rome had a profound effect on most of western Europe, where the Roman Empire had once seemed invincible. In addition to the Goths, other groups of traveling barbarians were also threatening all other major Roman territories. As noted historian Geoffrey Ashe describes,

> From the Atlantic to the Adriatic the Roman Empire was crumbling. Predatory barbarians were in Gaul [present-day central France] and Spain as well as in Italy. They were not conquerors, not yet, for no territory had been signed away to them. But they were there, unassimilated and menacing: not only the Goths but other alien peoples—Franks, Vandals, Alans, Suevi. Saxons and Burgundians were on the move. From over the Eastern plains came the most alarming barbarians of them all, the Huns, who had pushed some of the Goths across the frontier and were soon to push across it themselves. On the face of it a battered society was dying.[8]

Indeed, nothing seemed secure anymore for Rome and its provinces.

Britain too was affected by the marauding hordes that plagued fifth-century Europe. Until 410, Britain was a Roman province. Under Roman rule, the Britons enjoyed the wealth and security of the Roman Empire. The leadership of the Romans led to the construction of roads and buildings such as temples and bath houses. Roman leadership also built stone forts so soldiers could protect themselves from foreign attackers. Furthermore, the

The Romans built numerous roads, buildings, and forts during their occupation of Britain.

Britons identified with the leadership of the Romans, including their capital on the Continent, Rome itself. However, because of the Roman Empire's weakened state of affairs, Rome withdrew its troops from Britain, leaving the Celtic Britons to fend for themselves. From 410 until 440, in the wake of the pullout of Roman forces, Britain also began to endure devastating barbarian attacks from three groups of people, the Picts and the Scots from the northernmost part of the British Isles and, most notably, the Saxons, who landed by boat on the southern shores of Britain.

Britain Before Arthur

In response to the ongoing invasions, a weak and disorganized British ruling council turned to their former rulers, the Roman Empire, to ask for help, but the Roman government was unable or unwilling to offer what resources they still had. With no central leadership capable of maintaining the former territories of the Roman province, individual British warlords began to assume power—and to fight each other in the process. So, even as the barbarian attacks continued, the people of Britain also underwent a period of civil war not unlike the one described by Malory between the duke and King Uther in *Morte D'Arthur*.

From A.D. 440 to 450, local tyrants fought to divide the country between them while also seeking to defend their lands from others. Most Britons suffered heavily due to the constant warring: Farms were raided and burned; residents caught within the fighting were killed; and remaining food stocks were destroyed or stolen, causing a famine which only worsened the horrors the Britons experienced. To compound the already desperate situation, thousands of Saxons arrived from the Continent and landed on Britain's southern shores in 452. They raided towns and cities and took a piece of the island as their own. By all surviving accounts, these were desperate times for the Britons.

Yet perhaps what is most striking about the Britons was their resilience against these invaders. Despite the adversities they faced, the Britons of pre-Arthurian times managed to prevent the Saxons from completely taking over the island by organizing themselves into fighting groups to protect their families and neighbors. Ashe suggests that some of the resiliency of the Briton identity may have resulted from the Britons being allowed to maintain a distinctive Celtic-Briton identity even while under Roman rule. But even without the Romans, the Britons felt that they were one people and that the British Isles belonged to them. Ashe also surmises, however, that most of the British resilience was probably due to the memory of better times when Britain was a Roman province; under Roman rule, the Britons had enjoyed a measure of success unmatched by their barbarian foes.

Because of these positive memories under Roman rule, the Britons hoped to be able to defeat the invading Saxons and ensure a strong future. This belief was fueled further by a continuing faith in what "Eternal Rome" represented, the idea that a strong leader could unify their people once more. A leader, known as a restitutor or restorer, could potentially reunite and solidify their territory. As Ashe explains,

Maintaining a distinct identity under Roman rule helped the Britons become resilient in difficult times.

In the late fourth century and the first few years of the early fifth, rhetoric about Eternal Rome, as an idea or symbol, was louder than ever. But the mystique survived in a tangle of divided wills, unsolved problems, heavy and growing pressures from within

Britons faced the Saxon invaders alone after Rome withdrew from Britain.

and without. A *Restitutor* to pull everything together and reaffirm the ideal could still be dreamed of, and with more yearning because of the needs of the time. No one could tell where he might come from, or how he might act if he came.[9]

It is clear that Britain experienced turmoil until the end of the fifth century. But what of Arthur himself, and how did he become the legendary restitutor we know of today? Interestingly, the trail to Arthur does not begin with him at all but with another resistance leader, and a Roman one at that.

Ambrosius Aurelianus

With the Saxons invading Britain from the south and the Britons themselves undergoing tumultuous times, it is not hard to imagine that the Britons would follow a leader who could guide them to relative stability. Although it may seem surprising that the leader who emerged was Roman, it was also indicative of the times, as elements of Roman rule continued to affect post-Roman Britain. Despite the fact that the Roman Empire withdrew its forces in the mid–fifth century, Rome did remain in the minds of both the Britons and the Romans who chose to stay behind. One of those Romans was Ambrosius Aurelianus.

Little is known about Ambrosius, but it is known that he was a landholder in southern England during Arthur's era. In its basic sense, the title of landholder simply means a military chief who possessed regional power; however, this title also translates into the much more polite and prestigious title of prince. That Ambrosius controlled forces capable of fighting the Saxons seems certain.

This information was discovered in one of the very few surviving manuscripts of Arthur's era titled *The Ruin and Conquest of Britain,* written by Gildas, a British monk who lived in the sixth century. *The Ruin and Conquest of Britain* is not a straightforward historical text but a religious document in which Gildas spends much time condemning contemporary and past rulers for their immoral behavior. However, despite his inconsistencies, Gildas provides the most intact and voluminous account of an otherwise sparsely documented era. As such, Gildas remains one of the best sources available to which scholars have been able to turn in their efforts to reconstruct a history of fifth- and sixth-century Britain. One account by Gildas relates some specific information about Ambrosius.

When the Saxons were forced to withdraw to their home bases, Ambrosius Aurelianus, who Gildas calls "the last of the Romans," launched a counteraction from his lands in southern Britain. A number of battles were waged, and both the Saxons and Ambrosius's forces suffered wins and losses. Finally, in approximately A.D. 500, Ambrosius was able to claim victory after a great battle at the site of Mount Badon in which he survived a siege. The Saxons surrounded one of his fortresses and cut off supply routes to attempt to force a surrender. The siege, however, was ineffective, because the Britons were able to hold out longer than the Saxons. As the disheartened Saxon army turned to leave, Ambrosius's forces launched a well-orchestrated counterattack on the Saxon horde and defeated them.

Historians and archaeologists have attempted to verify Gildas's account of the Battle of Mount Badon by locating a number of likely sites for the siege based on the assumption that the battle was indeed fought in south Britain. Because a siege would require a fort in good working order, archaeologists have sought to locate a fort in approximately the right place at approximately the right time. The best

Historians and archaeologists search for evidence to verify the accounts of the Battle of Mount Badon.

candidate they have managed to unearth is located in Wiltshire. Ashe provides more detail:

> An ancient hill fort in Wiltshire, Badington Castle, has a village of Badbury close by and is a good candidate. Excavation has shown that its earthwork ramparts were refurbished at about the right time. A British force could have dug in there, endured a Saxon siege, and then routed a discouraged enemy in a sortie [raid]. The same could have happened on a hill near Bath which has also been proposed.[10]

What historians find truly exciting about finding evidence of the Battle of Mount Badon is that it also provides the first clues to the possible existence of King Arthur. Though Gildas does not mention Arthur at all, other later texts attribute the victory of Mount Badon to Arthur himself; as a matter of fact, it is supposed to be one of Arthur's greatest triumphs.

The fact that Gildas does not include Arthur in his description of the Battle of Mount Badon is less surprising than it may seem. Gildas was by no means an objective historical narrator. Because he was interested in using history to preach his message of Christianity, some historians have suggested that Gildas may have excluded any figures that he would have perceived to be unimportant. This would have included Arthur because Gildas would not be interested in commending the Britons for leadership. Instead, Gildas sought to highlight only the successes of the old Rome, which Ambrosius symbolized. As Ashe explains,

> Gildas names only one Briton throughout the fifth century and early sixth, Ambrosius. The trouble with this cleric is that he is exhorting, he is not writing history for its own sake. He regards most Britons as unworthy to be commemorated. . . . [Gildas's] silence about Arthur is not an argument

against [Arthur's] reality, though some modern writers have tried to make it so. . . . With an original Arthur, he might have been silent because of his prejudices, or because of a gap in his information.[11]

So even though one person may have contributed greatly to the defeat of the Saxons, Gildas may or may not have mentioned him. This may have included Arthur.

Regardless, the evidence provided by Gildas's manuscript is inconclusive and by itself would not be enough to substantiate the actual existence of an Arthur. However, other sources have provided additional clues to Arthur's existence and to the role he may have played both alongside and after Ambrosius.

Finding Arthur

Although records of Arthur are sparse at best, historians have been able to make a case for his existence. Most significant is that there are records of Arthur at all, however skewed or altered they might be. After the retreat by Roman forces (with the exception of a notable few such as Ambrosius), the Britons' struggle with invading peoples made the completion and preservation of written records almost impossible. As a result, early-fifth-century Britain became almost a blank page in history. Given this historical blackout, it is amazing that the memory of one Briton, Arthur, should survive at all.

Most historians agree that the preservation of Arthur's legend is a testament to the existence of *someone* by that name who had a profound impact on the post-Roman Britons. As the Arthurian scholar Norma Goodrich explains,

As the native Celtic peoples recovered and began to move again and fight over the ruins and the spoils, paying some obedience to those noble Romans who had nowhere else to go and who therefore had stayed in Britain, the Saxon invasions began in earnest. There was virtually no one to stop the Vikings, immigrants and land-hungry farmers from Scandinavia and the continent. The largest bloc of Anglo-Saxon colonizers clashed heavily with the native Celtic peoples. All struggled for footholds, livings, farmlands, and real estate. The only person to make a name for himself in all this turmoil was King Arthur. For that reason his role and his case seem unique in the history of the world.[12]

Another clue to the likelihood of the legendary king's existence also deals with his name. The name *Arthur* is not of Celtic origin and is therefore not a Briton name at all. Most scholars agree that Arthur is probably derived from the Roman name *Arturius,* which would make sense given the recent Roman occupation of Britain.

Furthermore, although records detailing the late fifth and early sixth centuries are scarce, a number of sources did become more available after the year A.D. 550, including those that detail the births and lineages of some noble houses. Despite the fact that most Roman names vanished at the end of the fifth century, there was a mysterious resurgence of the name *Arthur.* As Ashe explains,

> With this particular Roman name [Arthur], something unusual happened. It enjoyed a brief revival. In the decades after 550, despite the general vanishing of Roman names, at least four Arthurs are on record in the princely houses in Wales and Scotland. Such an out-of-line choice by at least four sets of parents, a long way apart, points to a common inspiration at work—the widespread fame of a prototype living somewhat before: a man after whom it was natural, patriotic perhaps, to name boys.[13]

Numerous texts mention Arthur or an Arthur-like person leading the Britons into battle against invading Saxon armies.

This has led a number of historians to theorize that some person named Arthur must have existed just prior to the year 550 and that he was someone important to the people of Britain. Of course, simple inference would not be enough to substantiate the existence of King Arthur. Historians have also had to analyze in painstaking detail those limited records that do remain.

Traces of Arthur

A number of ancient texts have mentioned an actual Arthur or Arthurian-like figure who led the Britons into battle against the invading hosts of Saxons. A few poems from about the same time as Gildas's account mention Arthur by name; one calls him *ameraudur*, the Latin equivalent of either "commander-in-chief," which was more common, or "emperor."

Another Welsh poem from a medieval collection titled *The Black Book of Carmarthen* makes reference to Arthur's men:

> In Llongborth I saw Arthur's
> Brave men who cut with steel,
> The emperor, ruler in toil of battle.[14]

Though this poem was written around the eighth century, approximately three hundred years after the battle it recounts, historians argue that the origin of the poem may even predate Gildas and probably is a new version of another older poem. But these are just hints, clues that provide no real substance in the effort to put together a vision of an actual Arthur or the role he may have played in the history of Britain. One other source, however, gives us a bit more to go on.

One of the most authoritative testaments to Arthur is a large and disorganized collection of manuscripts that were written in the early ninth century, more than four hundred years after the real Arthur would have lived. Historians tentatively attribute the work, called the *Historia Britonum (History of the Britons)*, to an obscure monk of northern Wales named Nennius. The *Historia Britonum* is one of the first records to refer directly to Arthur by name and deed.

This work of Nennius is a disorganized collection that is difficult to wade through and even more difficult to translate. But it is because of its disorganization that historians give the *Historia Britonum* as much authority as they do. As Ashe confesses,

> [Nennius] put together a jumble of materials, "making one heap," in his own disarming words, "of

all he found." The result is chaotic. Yet the chaos inspires a kind of trust. He is so plainly not a literary artist that we can believe he is quoting real traditions and early records. He hardly seems capable of making them up.[15]

In the *Historia Britonum*, Nennius tells about Arthur's twelve legendary battles in a passage thought to be an adaptation of a long lost Welsh poem. Though many of the battles cannot be confirmed, one battle Nennius refers to is the defeat of the Saxons at the Battle of Mount Badon, which historians suspect to have occurred and

Gildas felt that the Roman landholder Ambrosius Aurelianus defeated the Saxons at the Battle of Mount Badon, while Nennius attributes this victory to Arthur.

which Gildas attributes to Ambrosius. Nennius, however, has almost nothing to say about Gildas's Roman landholder. Instead, his detailing of the battles with the Saxons offers another restitutor:

> Then Arthur fought against [the Saxons] in those days with the kings of the Britons, but he himself was [the] leader in battles. The first battle was at the mouth of the river called Glein. The second and third and fourth and fifth upon another river which is called Dubglas and is in the district Linnuis. . . . The twelfth battle was on Mount Badon, in which nine hundred and sixty men fell in one day from one charge by Arthur, and no one overthrew them except himself alone. And in all the battles he stood forth as victor.[16]

Despite the fact that this record is one of the only confirmations that Arthur did indeed fight against the Saxons, how much does Nennius really say? Even if the obvious exaggerations—that Arthur killed more than nine hundred men single-handedly, for example—are discarded, we are still left to guess at Arthur's actual role in the fights. He seems to be Britain's war leader, but in what position? Is he fighting with other kings simply as a commander-in-chief? Is he working for Ambrosius or alongside him? Or is he the actual high king of the Britons as legend would have us believe?

Unfortunately for us, Nennius simply assumes that his readers know who Arthur is and therefore provides no confirmation. However, more clues can be found by looking at what type of army Arthur would have had under his command.

A Very Different Army

The traditional image of the Arthurian knights riding into battle while wielding lances and wearing full-body armor is

not accurate. In the fifth century, no culture, not even that of the Romans, possessed the metal skills necessary to construct such sophisticated weaponry. These romantic additions were instead the inventions of writers such as Sir Thomas Malory who came much later. Yet if Arthur did exist as either a king or a commander of some larger force, he would have had to have an army. A fifth-century army provides hints at the kind of person Arthur probably would have been if he did exist.

It is known that the Romans had a rough equivalent to the medieval knight. These knights were called *equites,* which translates as "horsemen." They were a social class of warrior who functioned as the Roman cavalry and played a major role in the war campaigns conducted by Rome in their final centuries of existence. These *equites* wore mail, a form of armor made of adjoining metal rings, and they wielded both spears and swords.

Because Britain was a Roman province until just before Arthur's time, historians have suggested that a British cavalry could have been based on this Roman model. If Gildas's account of the Britons led by Ambrosius is true, the probability of the Roman model army seems even more likely. Furthermore, Britain probably maintained contacts with the Roman forces on the Continent in Gaul, in present-day

It is likely that Arthur's knights were really Roman equites.

France, as roads and shipping routes used for trading continued to be used by both the Britons and the Romans. This contact with Roman forces substantially strengthens the theory that the Britons would have had access to Roman weapons and battle techniques. As Jack Lindsay explains,

The Britons may have used Roman armor and weapons against the Saxon invaders.

The Roman party in Britain were certainly in contact with Gaul and would know a good deal about the army methods and systems of the imperial [Roman] government. Though there had been heavy setbacks, the amount of crafts-skills still available in the area . . . must have been large. There would be no difficulty in turning out effective chain armor and the other paraphernalia of the cavalry troops of the imperial army.[17]

In addition, numerous records detail how the Romans dealt with barbarian invaders elsewhere in Europe. From these records, we can construct a probable strategy for the Britons. The invading forces, including the Saxons, were not as well equipped as the Romans and their Briton counterparts; the Saxons would not have possessed the Romans' superior weaponry or armor, and they did not use horses in battle. A well-armed and -armored cavalry, therefore, could more easily overwhelm the slower and more vulnerable invading barbarians. As early as the fourth century, the Roman commanders in Britain commanded on average twice as many cavalry units as foot soldiers. There is little reason to assume that, given the comparatively recent Roman connections with Britain, these tactics were not still in use. A real Arthur would have had a Roman cavalry and Roman connections.

The final issue is Roman leadership. Gildas's account places Ambrosius at the Battle of Mount Badon. But what about Arthur? Norma Goodrich seeks to answer this question by returning to the issue of Arthur's ancestry. According to Goodrich, based on the derivation of the name *Arthur* from the Roman *Arturius,* a real King Arthur would have probably been, in part, of Roman descent. Combining this information with the assumption that Arthur was also a great warrior of high birth, Goodrich surmises that a true-to-life Arthur would have in all likelihood experienced the training that all other Roman war leaders would have had. Furthermore, in later manuscripts, including those of Nennius, Arthur seems to have earned the title of "noble Roman." As Goodrich argues,

> Since Arthur is customarily called "noble Roman" (Queen Guinevere is also so called), Arthur must have been born inside the ancient Roman province, probably near some Roman installation, such as a training camp for British recruits. Chances are that he was educated nearby and that the proximity of the training camp was the key; King Arthur . . . was highly trained as a field officer in his youth.[18]

A real Arthur, therefore, would have probably enjoyed the benefits not only of a Roman-style cavalry but Roman-style tactics and training as well. This presumed combination would have been deadly for the Saxons at Mount Badon. Such a victory would surely have secured Arthur's fame as a great war leader.

General or King?

It seems likely that a person named Arthur did exist and that he was probably a great war leader. But was he really a king? The concept of kingship existed for the Britons of the fifth century, so kings did exist. Geoffrey of Monmouth, a cleric and historian who wrote almost six hundred years after Arthur's era, claimed that Arthur was actually the relative and successor of the Roman Ambrosius. If this was true, then Arthur would have possessed legitimate blood ties to the leadership of Britain. He could even have been a landholder or prince himself.

Arthur could have also solidified his claim to kingship with an overwhelming victory at Mount Badon. With the arrest of the Saxon invasion, it is possible that Arthur could have unified the Britons under his reign now that peace existed once again. Since it is known that the Britons were

comparatively trouble-free for approximately forty years after the Battle of Mount Badon, this implies some sort of successful central leadership.

Some historians feel that Arthur was merely a local commander with great military skill.

More recent historians have also argued for Arthur's relation to Ambrosius, which would imply some sort of regal status for Arthur, perhaps even the title of king. But others differ sharply. Ultimately, there are two schools of thought: those who believe that Arthur was a local commander with obvious great skill—but not a king—whose name subsequently became inflated by legend, and those who argue that Arthur was indeed a wide-ranging and kingly commander of Roman descent who managed to reunite and hold the territories of the former Roman province of Britain. Most historians, unwilling to draw a firm conclusion, simply take the middle ground by claiming that the truth will probably never be known. As Lindsay writes,

Arthur may have been [a king of kings] or he may have been a special sort of war chief who was supreme in whatever part of Britain he was carried by the war needs. . . . On the whole, it is best to consider Arthur a brilliant general who won his reputation under Ambrosius and who was entrusted with an over-riding commission during a period of pressing danger from the Saxon invaders.[19]

It seems that it is impossible to say for sure whether Arthur did achieve the kingship upon which his legend rests. Indeed, historians may never be able to determine the truth of this matter. But perhaps what is more perplexing is that writers like Malory probably had even less evidence to go on than modern scholars do. Yet Malory's history is so detailed that one must wonder how such a complicated and complete history of the legend of King Arthur could have possibly evolved.

Chapter 3

The Romantic Evolution of Arthur

Given that there are obvious contradictions between Sir Malory's Arthurian legend and the very few actual facts that can be traced to the historical figure of Arthur, perhaps what is most confusing about the mystery of the fabled king is how the romantic vision of *Morte D'Arthur* came to exist as such a complex compilation of stories. The trail of Arthur's saga is a long one, and traces of the legends can be found in stories from all over Europe. And despite the fact that the initial legends are firmly rooted within the traditions of the British Isles, most of these legends did not originate in the English language at all but in Latin and French.

To uncover the secrets to the survival and changing image of Arthur, it is best to begin an exploration of Arthur's revival in the Celtic oral histories. The legend then traveled to Europe, in what is now present-day France, where it was further enhanced by a number of storytellers. It was these later additions that directly affected Malory's own retellings of Arthur in *Morte D'Arthur* in English, nearly one thousand years after the existence of the fabled king.

Merlin and Excalibur

Much of the Arthurian legend was first preserved as an oral history, meaning that individuals memorized and retold the stories of King Arthur instead of writing them down. Originally, the Celtic people of Wales and Cornwall, descendants of the original Britons, guarded the Arthurian tales as their own. In fact, until 1137 when the monk Geoffrey of

Many of the magical elements in the Arthurian legends come from the Celtic belief in fairies and otherworld personalities.

Monmouth wrote in Latin the earliest known complete Arthurian history, there were hardly any written records at all.

Celtic history is a conglomeration of fact and fiction, both of which played an important role in how the Celts identified with the world around them. Their myths derived mainly from a belief in otherworld personalities, notably the fairy world that they believed existed alongside their own. The Celts believed that many of these fairies lived within the natural world around them. Trees, rivers, and even lakes were said to be inhabited by these spirits. Sometimes they would harm humans. If they assisted a human, there was almost always a trade involved. Even after Christianity arrived from the Roman Empire in the second and third centuries, the Celts managed to preserve their mythology by incorporating both sets of beliefs into their daily lives.

The tale of Excalibur, King Arthur's magic sword, derives from this tradition, as does the existence of Merlin; both hint at a supernatural and magical world typical of Celtic oral histories. In most versions of Arthur's finding of Excalibur, including that of Malory's *Morte D'Arthur*, Arthur is traveling through the British countryside in the company of Merlin when he gains the sword. Arthur is defenseless because his old sword has been broken in a prior battle from which he barely escaped. Merlin, however, is wise to the ways of the supernatural and promises Arthur a sword worthy of his crown.

During their return to Camelot, Merlin leads Arthur to a lake. Arthur is surprised by what he sees in the middle of the lake: an arm holding a great sword thrusting through the surface of the water. With Merlin at his side, Arthur is approached by the Lady of the Lake, who is the owner of the sword. The lady agrees to give Arthur the sword, called Excalibur, but in return she demands the right to ask a favor of Arthur whenever she pleases. Arthur agrees and

Accompanied by Merlin, Arthur rows to the middle of a lake to obtain Excalibur, his magic sword.

rows a boat to the center of the lake to retrieve the sword. As Malory describes,

Anon withal came the damosel unto Arthur, and saluted him, and he her again. Damosel, said Arthur, what sword is that, that yonder the arm holdeth above the water? I would it were mine, for I have no sword. Sir Arthur king, said the damosel, that sword is mine, and if ye will give me a gift when I ask it you, ye shall have it. By my faith, said Arthur, I will give you what gift ye will ask. Well! said the damosel, go ye into yonder barge, and row yourself to the sword, and take it and the scabbard with you, and I will ask my gift when I see my time.

So Sir Arthur and Merlin alit and tied their horses to two trees, and so they went into the ship, and when they came to the sword that the hand held, Sir Arthur took it up by the handles, and took it with him, and the arm and the hand went under the water.[20]

With the taking of the sword, Arthur is provided with yet another confirmation of his glorious destiny, only this time by the supernatural forces taken from his Celtic beginnings.

Geoffrey of Monmouth

As time progressed, early historians sought to write down the tales of Arthur. In A.D. 1137, roughly four centuries after the existence of the real Arthur, Geoffrey of Monmouth scribed in Latin the *Historia regum Britanniae (History of the Kings of Britain)*. Little is known about Geoffrey other than that he was a cleric and almost certainly a teacher who also possessed a failed appointment as bishop of Saint Asaph in Wales. He was also a self-proclaimed historian who sought to pen the lineage of British kings from pre-Arthurian times to Arthur's era.

The *Historia* details British history beginning about 1200 B.C. It describes the reign of seventy-five kings, most of whom we now know to be inventions of Geoffrey's own vivid imagination. Geoffrey was not content simply compiling what information was available, most notably from the accounts of Gildas and the work of another historian, the Venerable Bede's *History of the English Church and People*. Instead, Geoffrey combines these more factual accounts with the oral traditions and legends of the Celts and with other mythologies as well, including those of the Greeks and the Romans. But Geoffrey was most fascinated by the legend of Arthur, and despite the fact that the *Historia* spans over two thousand years, more than half of

Geoffrey's volume deals with the exploits of the legendary king.

Geoffrey cites as his primary source an ancient handwritten text that he claimed was written by Merlin. Therefore, working with a unique and unprecedented source, Geoffrey introduced his contemporaries to the initial tales of Arthur, Merlin, Guinevere, and some of the more fabled knights. Since no one then or now has ever viewed this ancient source, the validity of Geoffrey's *Historia* was questioned even during his own time. As Michael J. Curley, author of *Geoffrey of Monmouth*, explains,

> Geoffrey has become so integral to our understanding of Arthurian literature, that we forget how controversial his history originally was. From its appearance in the midtwelfth century to the present day, the *History of the Kings of Britain* has aroused strong emotions. Many of Geoffrey's fellow historians were clearly stung by the way his work eclipsed their own. Upon being shown a copy of Geoffrey's *History of the Kings of Britain* at the monastery of Bec in 1139, Henry of Huntingdon stated that he was stupefied to see this great book because his own inquiries about the history of Britain from the time of its settlement by Brutus down to the invasion of Julius Caesar had turned up no information whatsoever, either written or oral.[21]

Modern scholarship has continued these allegations. Geoffrey apparently also lifted, reorganized, and substantially altered information from the works of Nennius and others. Furthermore, most historians assume that Geoffrey's source from Merlin was a fictive invention that Geoffrey created to provide his *Historia* with more credibility. Merlin himself was an impossible character in a supposedly true history of England: He casts spells, foretells the future, and ultimately through the magical transformation of Arthur's father, orchestrates Arthur's birth between Uther and Igraine, two people who had never been mentioned in previous surviving accounts or records. But even given these doubts, Geoffrey's work enjoyed an unrivaled success. His bold style and sense of dramatic build gave Arthur and his legendary saga an allure that captured Geoffrey's medieval audience.

Nevertheless, Geoffrey's *Historia* had its limitations, primarily in regard to its accessibility to the people of England. The *Historia* was written in the medieval scholar's language of Latin, not in the common tongue of the English people. Therefore, Geoffrey's account could be

Geoffrey of Monmouth (with harp) attracted a medieval audience by combining historical accounts of Arthur with Celtic legends and other myths.

appreciated only by those who could read his work, select members of the upper classes and monastic orders. It was not until the Arthurian legends were translated into French, a more common language, that the everyday reader could enjoy the heroism and feats of the fabled Briton king.

Arthur Crosses to France

In 1155, almost twenty years after Geoffrey of Monmouth wrote his *Historia,* Wace, a Norman gentleman and poet who wrote under the patronage of the English Crown, took the liberty of translating it into French under the new title *Roman de Brut.* Wace's title translates as the *Romance of Brutus,* which alludes to the legacy of Britain's supposed founding by the Trojan Brutus, a presumed distant relative of Arthur.

It is not surprising that a French-speaking poet wrote under the commission of the English Crown. French was the language of both the English and French nobility during most of the Middle Ages. Furthermore, Wace lived in Normandy (now the northern portion of modern-day France), which was then controlled by the British Crown.

Wace, however, did far more than simply translate the *Historia.* Wace was a poet, not a historian. He was therefore more interested in communicating a riveting story about Arthur than in attempting to convey a historically accurate account. In other words, Wace wanted to create a poem that appealed to a wide readership. He enhanced the stories of Arthur presented in the *Historia* whenever he found it convenient in order to increase the adventure and romance of the Arthurian saga. In fact, the modern-day reader could hardly think of Arthur without the additions of Wace, particularly the fabled Round Table (a story he probably adapted from other Celtic folk traditions, most likely those of Ireland). Wace indirectly confesses his intentions in the *Roman de Brut:*

While translating the Historia *from Latin into French, Wace enhanced the* Arthur *character by adding several heroic qualities.*

During the long peace of which I speak—I know not whether you have heard of it—the wonders were demonstrated and the adventures were found which are so often related of Arthur that ehyr [since] have been turned into a fable. The tales of Arthur are not all lies nor are they true. So much have the story-tellers told and so much have the makers of fables fabled to embellish their stories that they have made everything seem a fable.[22]

As a result of Wace's interest in telling a good story rather than being historically accurate, he also took liberties with Arthur's character. In Geoffrey's *Historia*, Arthur is known for his victories and adventures, but not much is said about his character. In the *Roman de Brut*, however, Wace develops the character of King Arthur by adding a superhuman charisma and record of leadership. These romantic depictions of Arthur can be seen in the following translation of a section of the *Roman de Brut* in which Arthur's virtues are extolled:

> I will tell you about the good qualities of Arthur; about none of them will I lie. He was a most valiant knight, exalted and renowned. Toward the arrogant, he was pitiless; toward the humble, gentle and compassionate. Mighty and bold and conquering, liberal in his gifts, and generous. He never denied the appeal of the indigent, when it was within his means. He desired esteem and glory and that his deeds be remembered. Toward those in his service he was courteous, and bore himself nobly. As long as he lived and reigned, he surpassed all other princes in courtliness and nobility, in strength and generosity.[23]

Wace's Arthur is truly a king without comparison; he is a heroic figure who has earned his place in history through great deeds and an even greater sense of fairness. As Donald Maddox points out regarding this passage, "This portrait attributes to Arthur all the initiative, strength, bravado, generosity, and compassion that one might expect of a charismatic leader with a loyal following."[24]

Wace managed to turn Arthur into a popular figure whose story intrigued the romantic sentiments of his medieval contemporaries. His success was further heightened by a growing popular interest in the old Celtic cultures and tales. Because *Roman de Brut* effectively combined this interest in the Celts with contemporary interests such as chivalry, love, and Christianity, Wace's version of the tales of Arthur seemed to take on a life of their own.

As a result, the story of Arthur spread throughout Europe and beyond. As one medieval commentator wrote as early as 1170,

What place is there within the bounds of the empire of Christendom to which the winged praises of Arthur the Briton has not extended? Who is there, I ask, who does not speak of Arthur the Briton, since he is but little less known to the peoples of Asia than to the Britons, as we are informed by our palmers who return from the countries to the East? The Eastern people speak of him as do the Western, though separated by the breadth of the whole earth. Egypt speaks of him, and the Bosporus is not silent. Rome, queen of cities, sings his deeds, and his wars are not unknown to her formal rival Carthage. Antioch, Armenia, and Palestine celebrate his feats.[25]

With the work of Wace firmly rooted as the base for the mystique and intrigue of King Arthur in the French language, a host of new writers began to borrow from Wace's tales for subject material for their own writings. However, these new writers were not concerned with Geoffrey's historical relevance or Wace's conversion of Arthur into a heroic figure. These writers were the products of changing times in which the romantic notions of knighthood and knightly ideals were helping to transform the values of society; thus these writers sought to appeal to these new ideas.

A Changing Society

In English-controlled France and Britain, the priorities of medieval society were changing drastically in the mid– and late twelfth century. These changes were primarily due to the shift away from war as the borders of the medieval kingdoms became more solidified. Warriors were called on less and less to fight for the aristocracy, and the aristocracy, in turn, became more concerned with showing off their own prestige, wealth, and power.

Wanting an epic hero like the French Charlemagne, King Henry II (pictured) encouraged his court writers to develop the stories of King Arthur.

During Wace's era and after, Britain was ruled by the French-speaking Henry II. King Henry was able to solidify his power and regime through his marriage to Eleanor of Aquitaine and thus gained the majority of his lands in France. The king of Britain held more land, and therefore more wealth and power, than his rival, the king of France.

However, the king of France did possess one thing that Henry II did not, the story of a great French hero, Charlemagne, and a corresponding surviving epic poem titled the *Song of Roland*, which proclaimed French primacy over that of the English. For Henry II, the timing of Wace's *Roman de Brut* could not have been more welcome, because Wace offered the people ruled by King Henry II a hero that came before Charlemagne. Henry II therefore encouraged his court writers to follow the example of Wace by developing the stories of Arthur, also known as the Matter of Britain, to further advocate British superiority. Geoffrey Ashe confirms Henry II's motivations:

For Henry and his successors the Matter of Britain came as a welcome retort. It made them heirs of a greater sovereign earlier still—spiritually if not lineally. The realm they ruled had once been foremost in grandeur and civilization. King Arthur had presided over a chivalric utopia, and the romancers echoed Geoffrey (and, remotely, historical fact) in making him campaign and wield power on the Continent.[26]

Courtly Writers and the Courts of Love

However, there was also another side to the campaign to increase Arthur's popularity, the romanticism of the court of Henry II's wife, Eleanor of Aquitaine. The romanticism of Arthur, while certainly an important tool for King Henry II, also represented a common interest of the times. Themes of romanticism, love, and adventure were preferred by Eleanor and her surrounding nobility. These themes became part of a set of ideals called courtly love and were included within the poems and ballads of the courtly writers who entertained the nobility.

For the most part, Eleanor lived apart from her royal husband in her own castle in the region of Poitu, located in

Eleanor of Aquitaine wanted the Arthurian stories to focus on the ideals of courtly love.

present-day southwestern France. Eleanor possessed not only her own castle and court but also the financial resources to support her day-to-day needs. With constant warring temporarily confined to the past, the nobility enjoyed more and more time for leisure pursuits, including support of the literary arts and its artists. As such, Eleanor was able to finance writers and artists of her own choosing. And she financed those writers who could best present her and her court with tales of romantic courtly love.

The notion of courtly love embraced the ideal of the pure and chaste knight who would devote his name, his resources, and indeed his life, if necessary, to the wishes and honor of his chosen lady. This is not to suggest that the knight was either a suitor or a husband. Instead, the lady was probably married to someone above the knight in station; the knight therefore performed his acts of heroism selflessly and chastely. In short, the noble knight was expected to love his lady unconditionally; to not do so would result in a loss of honor presumably unfathomable to the knightly code of conduct.

These fictive knights were no longer warriors who fought for king and country but lovers of the highest degree who fulfilled quests or embarked on adventures only for the benefit of their respective ladies. Furthermore, often the knight and his lady broke the vow of chastity together, which almost always ended in some romantic and harrowing tragedy. However, these noble knights probably did not exist in real life at all, for the members of Eleanor's court were not warriors but nobility who were used to a very easy and rich lifestyle. The notion of the romantic knight was invented for their entertainment by the writers of Eleanor's court.

The choice of King Arthur and his knights as the courtly writers' subject material was of no great surprise considering the rise in popularity of the Arthurian legends

Pictured is an illustration from Chrétien de Troyes's Romance of King Arthur.

after the publication of Wace's *Roman de Brut*. But, given the courtly writer's desire to entertain, the writers were even less interested than Wace in providing any remotely factual accounts of Arthur and his knights. In fact, the courtly writers abandoned any and all pretext that their stories were factual. Instead, they blatantly made up stories of adventure about the knights and their famed king. No medieval writer of Eleanor's court did this better than the best known of the twelfth-century French romantics, Chrétien de Troyes.

Chrétien de Troyes

Chrétien is indeed the best known contributor to the Arthurian saga. Little is known about Chrétien personally, but this is hardly surprising considering the scattered and inconsistent records that have survived to the present day. It is perhaps more noteworthy that much if not all of his writings have managed to survive; it is certainly a testament to the skill with which Chrétien accomplished his art.

What is known is that Chrétien enjoyed the private patronage of Eleanor's daughter from her marriage prior to Henry II, the Countess Marie de Champagne. Eleanor's daughter was a more avid fan of the romantic tales than even her mother. Indeed, it seems that she hired Chrétien to write only for her, as she was in overt competition with the courts of her mother and those of her sisters. As Norma Goodrich explains,

> In 1170, Queen Eleanor retired to France, where she established courts at the several provincial capitals of her extensive domains. Her French daughters married and established courts at Troyes, at Bar-sur-Aube, and at Blois on the Loire River. Each vied with the other for the most famous authors of the day. The countess of Champagne won with her Chrétien de Troyes.[27]

In choosing Chrétien, Marie chose an experienced author who understood how to turn her demands for a fable about Lancelot into a masterful story.

Of Chrétien de Troyes's surviving manuscripts, five romances remain. These manuscripts are the first of their kind in that they present preserved multiple texts of Arthurian fiction by a single author. Within these romances, Chrétien, like the other court writers, invents stories about the fabled knights of the Round Table, most of which have directly affected more modern retellings of the exploits of Arthur and his knights. Chrétien did not retell the Arthurian stories of Wace and Geoffrey; instead, he used the Arthurian legend as a backdrop for his own fiction. In fact, one of the most famous Arthurian legends came from the imagination of Chrétien—the story of Lancelot and Guinevere's love affair in which both Queen Guinevere and Sir Lancelot betray King Arthur by giving in to their secret affections for each other. As Ashe explains,

Chrétien de Troyes created the story of Lancelot and Guinevere's love affair.

Under her [Marie's] aegis and direction the poet Chrétien de Troyes wrote a series of verse romances. These are the first known presentations of some of the characters and themes: Lancelot, for instance, and the Grail. In the preface to one of them, Chrétien says, "It is my pleasure to relate a matter quite worthy of heed concerning the King whose fame was such that men still speak of him far and near; and I agree with the opinion of the Bretons that his name will live on for evermore."[28]

Arthur's own romantic downfall shows Chrétien's profound influence on the development of the Arthurian tales as well as the love Eleanor's court had for the sublime and ultimate tragedy that could be provoked by breaking the ideals of courtly love. However, the efforts of the French writers had another very profound effect on the Arthurian legend: Their concentration on the knights and their exploits left their audience with a variety of contradicting tales. This included varying depictions of the personality and character of King Arthur—all of which tended to contradict the more heroic vision of both Geoffrey of Monmouth and the initial French translator, Wace.

Arthur's Changing Image

Prior to Chrétien de Troyes and his lesser-known contemporary writers, the character of King Arthur was, as proposed by Geoffrey of Monmouth and Wace, a regal and dynamic leader who unified and defended England with deftness and compassion. However, because of the influence of the French romantics, Arthur's prestige was lessened. He was no longer always the just leader of the warriors of the Round Table. In fact, often his image became so tarnished that he was portrayed as powerless.

Much of Arthur's changing image was a result of the romantic movement itself. Because the emphasis of the

Following Chrétien's example, many writers began to portray Arthur as a dark, depressed, and problematic figure.

romantic movement was on the noble knight and the idealization of courtly love, King Arthur himself was not the preferred subject matter for the stories of Chrétien and his fellow writers. Instead, they chose either to elaborate on the stories of the knights mentioned in Wace's translation or to invent new characters (such as Lancelot) that they wove into the existing Arthurian tales.

The result was that King Arthur became a background figure, and his character was changed to suit the demands of the writer. No one was more guilty of this than Chrétien himself. He often portrayed Arthur as an obscure king often depressed and rarely capable of living up to the idyllic behavior of his own knights. Donald Maddox explains Chrétien's negative influence on Arthur's image in more detail:

Chrétien produced five major romances in which the Arthurian court and a new, far more sedentary Arthur make an appearance only at intervals in order to witness the departure of knights in search of adventure or to herald their return with festive accolades. Apart from these moments, king and court recede into obscurity as the heroic intrigue comes into prominence.[29]

By the High Middle Ages, which included Sir Thomas Malory's era, the image of Arthur was even more blackened and incongruous. There was no longer one epic story that could include all of the different versions of King Arthur. As Maddox elaborates,

After Chrétien, many romances in verse and prose depict Arthur as a problematic figure who, depending upon which of the many texts is considered, is not uncommonly depressed, lethargic, hesitant, powerless, concupiscent, incestuous, short-sighted, or even apparently senile.[30]

There was, therefore, no single attitude or understanding toward the character of King Arthur. Indeed, Malory's challenge in writing *Morte D'Arthur* was to try to put the pieces back together while also rebuilding the image of Arthur as the ancient British king of renown.

Although Chrétien de Troyes and his contemporaries initially emboldened the saga of Arthur through their development of the stories, their efforts also muddled the continuity of the legend because their emphasis was not on compiling any one continuing record but on the invention of individual stories. This, compounded by the French romantics' idolization of knightly values and subsequent undermining of the character of Arthur, left the English of the High Middle Ages with a new dilemma, for the social and political climate in England changed drastically during this time.

However, despite these various inventions from the French romantics, Chrétien and his contemporaries still had a lasting effect on the development of the Arthurian legend. Furthermore, even though the characters of Lancelot, Guinevere, and even Arthur were substantially invented, there was still some plausibility to some of the characters. In an effort to uncover the truth behind the mystery of King Arthur, historians have also investigated King Arthur's knights, as well as the possible location of their home at Camelot.

Chapter 4

Arthur's Knights and the Last Battle

The legend of King Arthur is more than simply the tale of one man, however unique he may have been in the course of history. Part of the appeal of Arthur has always been that he comes to us with a world of contemporaries, each developed and lifelike, full of strengths and weaknesses, bright and dark moments. Perhaps of even greater significance is how important these characters were to the legendary king—they all influence the course of events that make up the Arthurian saga. That saga includes Arthur's rise to kingship and solidification of Britain; the search for the Holy Grail; and even the king's death at the hands of the evil Mordred, who attempts to seize Arthur's throne at Camelot.

If any one of these characters existed or if historians could locate the fabled Camelot, perhaps they would also find more signs of the mysterious Arthur himself. It is therefore not surprising that the search for King Arthur has led historians to investigate whether there is any truth behind the tales of Arthur's knights and queen. Archaeologists have also lent a hand in the search for Arthur's castle and home, Camelot, and the Round Table.

Merlin the Prophet

The Merlin of legend was more than the guardian of the young Arthur and the provider of the magic sword, Excalibur. He was also the prophesier, the advice giver, and perhaps he, like Arthur, was more than legend. There is evidence that suggests that the character of Merlin was based on a number of factual accounts, some of which may have involved real men of the Dark Ages.

Stories about a Merlin-like prophet appear in many of the earliest Arthurian texts, including that of Nennius, who is thought to have recopied a text of Welsh origin.

Archaeologists dig at a site believed to be the location of Camelot.

However, the authenticity of Nennius's account is immediately suspect because he writes of a nameless boy born from the union of a human woman and a demon. Although his mother had him baptized immediately upon his birth, thereby ridding the boy of potential evil, the boy retained otherworldly powers and knowledge, including the gift of prophecy. For example, the boy interprets the battle of two dragons—one red and one white—as the struggle between the Saxons and the Britons. He also foretells the initial defeat of the red (the Britons) until a future time when the Britons will rise again under Arthur.

The boy, however, does not assume the name *Merlin* until Geoffrey of Monmouth's *Historia regum Britanniae* in

Many historians consider Merlin to be a conglomerate of numerous real persons and characters from several early British poems.

The first time the name Merlin is used in Arthurian tales occurs during a conversation between King Vortigern (left) and Merlin in Geoffrey's Historia.

1137. In Geoffrey's version, the reigning king, called Vortigern, asks the boy his name after he explains the meaning of the dragons. The boy says that he is called Merlin Ambrosius. Geoffrey adds further details to the life of Merlin in both his *Historia* and another later work, a poem titled *Vita Merlini (The Life of Merlin)* completed between 1148 and 1155. According to Geoffrey, on reaching adulthood, Merlin becomes the prophet of South Wales. After the death of Arthur, Merlin goes mad and takes to the woods after witnessing a particularly gruesome battle. When he recovers, he returns from the wilderness and predicts the return of Arthur.

Although Geoffrey invents Merlin in many respects, he also "borrows" not only from Nennius but also from other sources, most notably a collection of poems and records called *The Lailoken Fragments* and a body of Welsh poetry called *The Welsh Myrddin Poems*. It is in reference to these latter two sources that historians have argued for the possibility of a "real" Merlin (or more than one) who became the basis for Geoffrey's character.

The Lailoken Fragments tells of a north British wild man called Lailoken who is discovered in the woods by Saint Kentigern, the patron saint of Glasgow. Like Merlin, Lailoken also went mad at the sight of a battle, and he too displayed the gift of prophecy. As author Michael Curley summarizes,

> Asked by the saint to explain his presence [in the woods], Lailoken tells how he was driven into the wilderness by a voice that came to him from the sky during a battle and that blamed him for the carnage that day. The story relates the deep sympathy that Kentigern felt for Lailoken in his harsh life in the wilderness; it also contains a version of the three-fold death which Lailoken predicts for himself (to be killed by stones and clubs, pierced by a sharp stake, and drowned in water), and which comes true when he is set upon by the shepherds of King Meldred. He also predicts the death within a year of the King of Britain, the most holy of bishops, and the most noble of lords.[31]

The Welsh Myrddin Poems also could have provided Geoffrey with a historical model for the character of Merlin, one who would have lived around A.D. 540 to 630 just *after* Arthur's presumed life span. This historical Merlin was called *Myrddin Wyllt,* which translates as "Merlin the Wild" or "Merlin the Mad." He was a bard—a poet and storyteller who sang his works—of the ancient

Britons, and historians have attributed a few surviving poems to his authorship. But he was hardly the magical and otherworldly figure found in Geoffrey's or Malory's work. Furthermore, it is difficult to know exactly how much Geoffrey may have drawn from the *Myrddin* poems. As Curley explains,

> Discerning precisely what Geoffrey knew of the traditions concerning Myridin is difficult, partly because of his tendency to turn his sources to his own literary purposes . . . and partly too because the highly allusive Welsh poems concerning Myridin assume much knowledge on the part of the listener and are themselves fluid and sometimes contradictory.[32]

While Geoffrey may have used these sources in his own portrayal of Merlin, the character of the wizard was enhanced and romanticized continuously until he became almost purely fiction. The Merlin character of *The Lailoken Fragments* is murdered. The Merlin figure of Geoffrey ends his days living in a castle in the forest of north Britain. By Malory's time, the most romantic of the Merlins meets a much more tragic end—Merlin is lured to his death by a former student, Vivien. In the Britannic forest of Brocielande, Vivien sings an enchanted song that causes Merlin to fall into a deep sleep beneath a

In Malory's Morte D'Arthur *Merlin meets his tragic end when Vivien lures him into a deep sleep under a thorn tree.*

thorn tree, where she builds a tower of air in which she imprisons Arthur's magician indefinitely.

Lancelot

Historians have also searched for evidence of the existence of the most famous of Arthur's knights, Sir Lancelot. Lancelot makes his first appearance in Arthurian literature in a verse poem titled simply *Launcelot*, written by Chrétien de Troyes. The tale itself is traditionally thought of as a work of fiction with no basis in historical fact. But through a study of the legend, scholars have been able to uncover possible links between the highly romantic and fictive Lancelot and a historical figure.

It has long been assumed that the romance between Lancelot and Guinevere was the product of Chrétien under the thematic guidance of Marie de Champagne. As Norma Goodrich explains,

> The circumstances behind *Launcelot* and its composition are known and can be reconstructed with some accuracy. The work was commissioned by the countess Marie de Champagne, who supplied [Chrétien] with two resources: (1) the material of the account and (2) her wishes regarding the form of narration and the interpretation.[33]

The development of the highly romantic depiction of Lancelot was probably due to Marie's insistence and invention. Lancelot became the ideal knight of the courts of love and, as such, is handsome, daring, and devoted to his lady, Queen Guinevere. This explanation is what accounts for one of Lancelot's more telling episodes in which he demonstrates his devotion to Arthur's queen by rescuing her from the knight Sir Meliagante.

Meliagante so desired Guinevere for his own that he kidnapped her. Lancelot pursued Meliagante to the far-off kingdom of Gorre. When he reached the border of Gorre,

Lancelot found that a raging river blocked entry to the kingdom. The only way across was the Sword Bridge, a sword that stretched from bank to bank, its sharp edge facing up. To prove his love for the queen, Lancelot did the unthinkable and removed his armor from his hands and feet before crossing. He arrived at the other side horribly wounded, but still he prepared to battle Meliagante. The knights fought until the king of Gorre halted the battle. A truce was made on the condition that Lancelot and Meliagante would fight again in one year, and Guinevere was released. On the day of the fight, after escaping from a trap laid by Meliagante, Lancelot fought his foe and struck him dead. Guinevere's honor was restored, and Lancelot had proved his devotion to his lady in true courtly fashion.

A fourteenth-century painting depicts Lancelot as he crosses the Sword Bridge during an adventure to rescue Guinevere from Meliagante.

Because Chrétien so obviously used Lancelot to entertain Marie and her court, Lancelot has been thought by most scholars to be a purely fictive construct of Chrétien's. Given the inventions of blatant impossibilities such as the Sword Bridge, Lancelot becomes an impossible character himself. But, as in the case of Arthur, it is possible that the writers of the Middle Ages based their impossible histories on historically accurate personas.

Goodrich has offered some evidence that may attest to an actual Lancelot and Guinevere; however, their love affair was probably an invention. Apparently, Chrétien may

Evidence suggests that Chrétien used several historical manuscripts to create the character of Lancelot.

have stumbled on a since-lost historical document that contained references to both Lancelot and Guinevere as historical figures of Britain during the Dark Ages. It seems likely that Chrétien would have had access to documents of this type if they did exist. As Goodrich explains with respect to the work of L. G. Ritchie,

> Chrétien, said Ritchie, had access to privileged information about the history of Scotland in the twelfth century and in the Dark Ages. He talks about the political realities that surrounded the reign of King Arthur in Strathclyde, at Carlisle, and at Dumbarton. He also knows accurate details

about the reign in Scotland of King David I. He probably got this information from the Augustinian or Austin canons at Jedburgh Abbey, Melrose Abbey, Holyrood Abbey, or Cambuskenneth Abbey in Stirling. . . . Chrétien admitted having taken one manuscript from Beauvis Abbey in northern France. The monks from Beauvis were the very administrators who helped King David I of Scotland reconstitute his abbeys inside Scotland. Chrétien talks about Saint Kentigern of Scotland, about King Arthur and his queen. . . . Furthermore, Chrétien wrote only fifty or so years after the reorganization by King David I of these same abbeys, where, reasonably, the archives of Scotland in the Dark Ages were most recently stored.[34]

Goodrich and others theorize that Chrétien used the content of these historical manuscripts as models for his characters in *Launcelot*. This would not be beyond Chrétien's ability or ingenuity. His verse *Launcelot* relies on a number of credible facts, including a fairly accurate and specific knowledge of Scotland and its political woes. It is possible, therefore, that a person like Lancelot may have existed and that he may have been devoted in some way to both Arthur and his queen.

Unfortunately, whatever sources Chrétien may have used are lost to modern scholarship. With Lancelot, as with so much of the mystery of King Arthur, the best that historians can do is guess. How much of Chrétien's *Launcelot* is based on truth and how much on his imagination will probably never be known for sure.

The Quest for the Holy Grail

Perhaps the greatest and most well known adventure of King Arthur's knights is the Quest for the Holy Grail. It is a lengthy affair full of adventure and piety in which all of

Arthur's knights journey away from Camelot in a desperate search for a sacred relic called the Grail.

What was the Grail? This is a difficult question to answer because the Grail changes shape and function throughout the developing history of its legend. In earlier versions, it is a silver plate, a magic stone, a drinking horn, or the cup from which Christ was supposed to have sipped during his last supper before being crucified. In one earlier tale, the Grail is a cauldron, or large cooking pot, into which Arthur gazes to see the future—only to uncover that the Grail also has the power to raise the dead.

In its more mature versions, however, the Grail is an ornamented chalice said to have caught the blood of Christ as he died upon the cross. Those who drank from the Grail would be healed of their wounds and sickness. Furthermore, one could be sustained by it indefinitely without food or drink.

According to legend, the Arthurian quest for the Holy Grail ends with its finding by Lancelot's only son, Sir Galahad. After many adventures and several encounters with near death, Galahad's quest leads him to the Grail Castle, a fortress said to appear in and out of mist, even to change locations from time to time. The Grail Castle is

The knights of the Round Table receive a blessing as they depart in search of the Holy Grail.

ruled by an old king, the Fisher King, who suffers from a wound that will not heal. Because of his goodness, Galahad is permitted to enter the chapel and kneel before the Grail. At the altar, Galahad prays for the Fisher King and his wound. Immediately, the Fisher King's wound is healed. However, as Galahad continues to gaze into the Grail, he finds that he has no desire to remain within this world. Sir Galahad is immediately transported to heaven.

Although the search for the Holy Grail during Arthurian times, in all likelihood, did not actually occur, historians believe that this mythical search was probably based on actual historical quests, albeit ones that occurred much later than the fifth or sixth centuries. During the thirteenth century, knights did embark on a number of crusades, militant pilgrimages in which Christian knights journeyed to Jerusalem and other holy cities either to take control of the city itself or to claim an artifact rumored to exist there. It is likely that these crusades were used as models for the developing legend.

The quest for the Holy Grail ends when Sir Galahad finds the Grail.

One alteration that is known to have occurred involved a group of French religious warriors called the Templar Knights who were engaged in a crusade that had a number of similarities to the Quest for the Holy Grail. The Templar Knights were the militant faction of the Cistercian

Order of monks and therefore wielded arms. They went on a quest for a piece of the "True Cross." Their order connected profoundly with the legends of the Arthurian Grail quest, and its leaders sought to make these connections even more apparent by rewriting the Arthurian legends with the Templar Knights as the model. As David Day explains,

The legend of the Holy Grail has many similarities to the quests of the Templar Knights.

The Templars saw themselves as knights in search of the Grail and their order consciously forged links with the legends of the Quest of the Holy Grail. Not only did they adapt aspects of the Grail Quest to suit their own rituals, but they actually wrote or rewrote the Grail legends to mirror and advocate the ideals of Templar Knighthood. . . . They transformed [the Quest of the Holy Grail] into a didactic allegory on the Christian doctrine of grace and salvation according to the teachings of the Cistercian philosopher Bernard of Clairvaux, and they aggressively employed the Grail Quest legend as a vehicle to advance the ideals of Templar Knighthood.[35]

Much of the detail provided for the Grail quest in the works of Chrétien and his contemporaries (as well as the work of later authors such as Malory) derived from the alterations of the Templar Knights. The Grail legend therefore most likely had its factual roots not in Arthurian Britain but in the Middle Ages of France. If the Templar Knights relied on an earlier Arthurian history, historians have not been able to locate any evidence of it. Historians have therefore been unable to prove whether a similar quest by Arthur's knights actually occurred during Britain's Golden Age or whether the legend of the Quest for the Holy Grail was a medieval invention.

Tintagel Castle

In the attempt to solve some of the mysteries of King Arthur, historians have also investigated the places and relics typically attributed to Arthur's reign. The Round Table and especially the castles, such as the fabled Camelot, could still exist if Arthur was indeed a fifth-century king. If historians could locate these artifacts, they would be one step closer to potentially locating some real traces of Arthur himself.

Arthur's birthplace has been one area where historians have worked with archaeologists to try to uncover historical proof of his existence. According to Geoffrey of Monmouth, Arthur was born and raised at Tintagel Castle, a coastal fort near Tintagel village. Many historians initially scoffed at this claim because the castle remains of Tintagel were built during Geoffrey's own era, five centuries after the period ascribed to King Arthur. They claimed that Geoffrey cited Tintagel Castle as Arthur's birthplace because he wanted to flatter the founder of the castle by slipping reference to it into his writings.

However, the archaeological efforts of C. A. Ralegh Radford have forced even the most stringent of critics to

Pictured are the remains
of Tintagel Castle, one
possible location of
Arthur's birthplace.

reconsider their opinions. Ashe describes the results of
Radford's excavations of Tintagel in detail:

Radford discovered what came to be called
Tintagel pottery. He dug up fragments of high-

quality vessels, of a type used for luxury goods such as wine. They had been imported from the eastern Mediterranean region, and could be dated to the latter part of the fifth century or the sixth. This imported ware gave the first major breakthrough into the "Arthurian" period in Britain. Somewhere hereabouts a wealthy household flourished at a date corresponding to the pottery and perhaps a little before—that is, in more or less "Arthurian" times.[36]

Though Radford established possible credibility to Geoffrey's claim, he could not prove that an "Arthur" once lived at the Tintagel site. The best he could manage was to show that someone of princely stature once lived there at about the right time. Thus, Geoffrey could have been relying on some older information which he had access to but modern historians do not.

Camelot and the Round Table

Other relics that have been historically ascribed to King Arthur, however, have not fared as well. Until relatively recently, Arthur's Round Table was thought to have existed at Winchester Castle in Wessex. At the end of the thirteenth century, Winchester was believed to have been the site of the real Camelot. Proof of this claim was Winchester's possession of the supposed Round Table itself: a solid oak table eighteen feet in diameter and weighing one and a quarter tons that is painted with alternating green and white spokes to mark a place for each of Arthur's knights.

The great table still hangs in the Great Hall of Winchester Castle to this day, and until the twentieth century it was presumed to be authentic. However, modern forensic science has exposed the table as a medieval forgery. Examinations of the wood from which the table was made revealed that the wood was cut just before A.D. 1250 during the reign of Edward I, seven hundred years after the presumed Golden Age of Arthur.

The potential location of Camelot has proved to be even more difficult, primarily because there are too many possibilities, none of which have provided any conclusive evidence that could substantiate such a claim. Despite the lack of a credible Round Table, Winchester Castle has continued to be a candidate for the location of Camelot. Other

For centuries it was believed that the table on display at Winchester Castle (pictured) was King Arthur's Round Table.

possible locations that have been put forth include Carlisle in Cumbria, Camelon in Scotland, Chester in the Midlands, Caerleon in Wales, Camelford in Cornwall, and Cadbury Castle in Somerset.

Interestingly, Goodrich suggests that the search for Camelot may be more elusive than pinpointing any one specific location. She begins by looking at the origins of the word *Camelot*, which, when broken down to its Latin derivatives, means "Castle of the Hammerer." "The Hammerer," she argues, would refer to Arthur himself. She argues that "Camelot" could have signified any castle where "the Hammerer" took up residence. Camelot therefore could have been a number of different locations throughout Arthurian Britain.

The Fall of a King

Another place historians have searched for evidence of King Arthur is the site of Arthur's final battle, a field somewhere in northeast Britain called Camlann. The Battle at Camlann represents not only the end of Arthur's reign but the end of a mythic and historic era. In the legend, Arthur returns to his kingdom to depose his nephew Mordred, the preemptor of his throne. In reality, Camlann signifies the end of the Britons' self-rule as the Saxon hordes return, this time successfully taking the island from the Roman-Celts.

According to legend, while warring against Lancelot because of his affair with Queen Guinevere, Arthur receives the news that his nephew, Sir Mordred, has revolted against him and claimed the throne. Arthur hastily gathers his forces together and retreats from Lancelot's lands in order to reclaim his kingdom. The battle between the two opposing armies is ferocious. At the battle's finale, only King Arthur and Sir Mordred are left standing and unwounded.

According to legend, Arthur's wounded body was taken away by the queens of the fairy realm after his final battle with Mordred.

Arthur grabs a spear and charges his spiteful nephew, running him through. But, before dying, Mordred delivers one last blow to his uncle. Hunched over the dead body of his nephew and attended by the last of his knights, Sir Bedivere, Arthur knows that he too is dying. Bedivere witnesses the arrival of a magical boat guided by the queens of

According to legend, Arthur's wounded body was taken away by the queens of the fairy realm after his final battle with Mordred.

the fairy realm. The queens take Arthur's still-living body away so that he might recover and one day return to rule England.

In support of the actual Battle at Camlann, historians point to a Welsh chronicle called the *Annales Cambriae (Annals of Wales)*. Compiled in A.D. 956, it gives the date of *A.D.* 539 for the battle. It also mentions that an Arthur and a Medreut (taken to be an early reference to Mordred) were slain there. It does not, however, make any mention of whether they were enemies or comrades, nor does it confirm a family relationship. These details would seem to be later additions of Geoffrey of Monmouth. In addition, the *Annales* do not give a precise location for the battle.

A number of different possibilities for its location have been proposed, including Cornwall and northern Wales. The most likely candidate, however, would appear to be on the northern border of sixth-century England at Camboglanna, a restored section of Hadrian's Wall, which was initially built and maintained by the pre-Arthurian Romans. Archaeological evidence suggests that this portion of the wall was restored at about the right time and that it was the location of one of the last stands of the Britons against their Saxon invaders. However, like so much of the mystery of King Arthur, even this is hardly conclusive. There are just too many pieces of the puzzle missing.

Scholars that do argue for a real Arthur's connection to the Battle at Camlann find themselves relying on the local folklore of Camboglanna to support their theories. As Goodrich describes,

> The death of King Arthur and of so many powerful personages is also remembered in this area, at and around what is today only the crumbling ruins of Sewingshields Castle, once a border town on

Pictured is Glastonbury Abbey, one of several sites that claim to be the location of King Arthur's grave.

Hadrian's Wall a short distance to the east of Camboglanna Fort. Folklore and local history both attest to this site as being where, in an underground crypt, the body of King Arthur was once laid.[37]

But still the mystery of Arthur's death lingers. Dozens of other locations have also claimed to be the final resting place of King Arthur. Each potential gravesite has been exposed either as impossible or indeterminable. While the memory of King Arthur has stood the test of time, the facts that support such a memory have remained elusive.

The Life of a King

The world of Arthur is such a mix of fantasy and reality that we will probably never be able to divulge all that is true or false about his presumed reign all those centuries ago. Since the changes in his story were often a mix of political motivations and the desire for entertainment confuses matters further. Historians would love to uncover the truth of what happened to the real Arthur. But as it stands, we will probably never have a solid answer.

What we do possess, however, is a powerful story that continues to affect our modern era despite its Dark Age beginnings. In modern England, the royal family still uses a sequence of titles that have their origins in their Middle Age fascination with Arthur. At birth, the prince is still baptized the duke of Cornwall after Arthur's supposed birthplace. And at the age of fifteen, he is crowned the prince of Wales because Arthur supposedly was chosen to rule the Welsh-Britons at that age.

Modern literature also proves that the allure of the Arthurian stories has not yet run its course. J. R. R. Tolkien used the Arthurian legend as one of his sources for his fictive trilogy, *The Lord of the Rings*. Marion Zimmer Bradley uses the Arthurian world in the plot of her novel *The Mists of Avalon*. Even the great twentieth-century poet T. S. Eliot refers to the Arthurian saga in his famous poem

Following Arthurian tradition, Prince Charles (pictured here at age seven) has held the title Duke of Cornwall since birth.

The Wasteland. And the hundreds of fantasy novels that dominate the shelves of bookstores today owe their beginnings, at least in part, to King Arthur and the authors who brought his great history to life.

Modern film has also paid tribute to this most infamous of English kings. In his *Star Wars* saga, George Lucas used King Arthur as a model for both Luke Skywalker and Obi-Wan Kenobi as well as the Jedi knights, and he continues to use these themes in his prequel trilogy. Steven Spielberg also took his turn at the Arthurian legend as he embraced the Grail quest and its allure in his film *Indiana Jones and the Last Crusade*. Even Walt Disney, with the comical cartoon *The Sword in the Stone*, used the legend to entertain and enthrall.

According to legend, Merlin foretold the return of Arthur in a prophecy in which he warned of the Bear (Arthur) who would return to loose his muzzle for war. Merlin presumably meant this prophecy as a threat to the Saxons. Yet despite the ferocity of Merlin's warning, King Arthur has continued to capture our interest and imagination

Obi-Wan Kenobi and other Jedi knights in the Star Wars *saga are based on King Arthur.*

through the centuries, from the manuscripts of Nennius and Geoffrey to even these pages here. Instead of being threatened by Arthur's return, perhaps we can simply overlook the warnings of Merlin as we appreciate the fact that, in one way, Arthur has never really left.

Notes

Chapter 1: From Boy to King

1. Geoffrey Ashe, *The Discovery of King Arthur.* New York: Anchor Press, 1985, p. 14.
2. Sir Thomas Malory, *Le Morte D'Arthur,* vol. 1. London: J. M. Dent & Sons, 1906, p. 7.
3. Malory, *Le Morte D'Arthur,* vol. 1, p. 8.
4. Malory, *Le Morte D'Arthur,* vol. 1, p. 10.
5. Malory, *Le Morte D'Arthur,* vol. 1, p. 11.
6. Malory, *Le Morte D'Arthur,* vol. 1, p. 71.
7. Malory, *Le Morte D'Arthur,* vol. 1, p. 71.

Chapter 2: Who Was the Real Arthur?

8. Ashe, *The Discovery of King Arthur,* p. 19.
9. Ashe, *The Discovery of King Arthur,* p. 24.
10. Ashe, *The Discovery of King Arthur,* p. 66.
11. Ashe, *The Discovery of King Arthur,* p. 68.
12. Norma Lorre Goodrich, *King Arthur.* New York and Toronto: Franklin Watts, 1986, pp. 14–15.
13. Ashe, *The Discovery of King Arthur,* p. 78.
14. Quoted in Ashe, *The Discovery of King Arthur,* p. 121.
15. Ashe, *The Discovery of King Arthur,* p. 68.
16. Quoted in Ashe, *The Discovery of King Arthur,* p. 69.
17. Jack Lindsay, *Arthur and His Times.* London: Frederick Muller, 1958, p. 216.
18. Goodrich, *King Arthur,* p. 50.
19. Lindsay, *Arthur and His Times,* p. 216.

Chapter 3: The Romantic Evolution of Arthur

20. Malory, *Le Morte D'Arthur,* vol. 1, p. 43.
21. Michael J. Curley, *Geoffrey of Monmouth.* New York: Twayne, 1994, p. ix.
22. Quoted in Ashe, *The Discovery of King Arthur,* p. 13.
23. Quoted in Donald Maddox, *The Arthurian Romances of Chrétien de Troyes.* Cambridge, England: Cambridge University Press, 1991, p. 2.
24. Maddox, *The Arthurian Romances of Chrétien de Troyes,* p. 2.
25. Quoted in Ashe, *The Discovery of King Arthur,* p. 168.
26. Ashe, *The Discovery of King Arthur,* p. 171.
27. Goodrich, *King Arthur,* p. 140.
28. Ashe, *The Discovery of King Arthur,* p. 169.
29. Maddox, *The Arthurian Romances of Chrétien de Troyes,* pp. 2–3.
30. Maddox, *The Arthurian Romances of Chrétien de Troyes,* p. 3.

Chapter 4: Arthur's Knights and the Last Battle

31. Curley, *Geoffrey of Monmouth,* p. 113.
32. Curley, *Geoffrey of Monmouth,* p. 115.
33. Goodrich, *King Arthur,* p. 128.
34. Goodrich, *King Arthur,* p. 138.
35. David Day, *The Quest for King Arthur.* London: Griffin House, 1995, p. 127.
36. Ashe, *The Discovery of King Arthur,* p. 78.
37. Goodrich, *King Arthur,* p. 265.

For Further Reading

Nonfiction

Roger Green, *King Arthur and His Knights of the Round Table*. New York: Puffin, 1996. A modern retelling of the key legends of King Arthur and his Knights of the Round Table as adapted from Sir Thomas Malory's *Le Morte D'Arthur*.

Mary Hoffman, *Women of Camelot: Queens and Enchantresses at the Court of King Arthur*. New York: Abbeville Press, 2000. Hoffman innovatively retells portions of the Arthurian legend from the points of view of the women involved in the saga, giving new voices and perspectives to the stories of Arthur and his court.

Martin Keatman and Graham Phillips, *King Arthur: The True Story*. Topeka, KS: Econo-Clad Books, 1999. Keatman and Phillips discuss evidence that they believe proves the theory that King Arthur was actually a Welsh warrior king called Owain Ddantgwyn.

Fiction

Marion Zimmer Bradley, *The Mists of Avalon*. New York: Ballantine Books, 1982. The author masterfully recreates the story of King Arthur, focusing on the magical saga of the women of the Arthurian legends.

Anne McCaffrey, *Black Horses for the King*. Orlando, FL: Harcourt Brace, 1996. Acclaimed author of popular fiction Anne McCaffrey gives a thrilling depiction of Artos (King Arthur) in this historical novel for younger audiences.

Mary Stewart, *The Crystal Cave*. New York: Fawcett Crest, 1970. The first in a series of three novels, this one delves into the life and personality of Merlin, the famed magician of Arthur's Camelot.

———, *The Hollow Hills*. New York: Fawcett Crest, 1973. The second in a series of three novels, this one tells the spellbinding story of how Merlin helped Arthur become king of Britain.

———, *The Last Enchantment*. New York: Fawcett Crest, 1979. The third in a series of three novels, this one reveals the sinister plots that threaten to destroy Arthur's reign in Camelot.

T. H. White, *The Once and Future King*. New York: Berkley Medallion Books, 1966. The classic novel, originally published in 1939, about the court of King Arthur and Arthur's upbringing under the guidance of the wizard Merlin. The author vividly recreates England of the Middle Ages and Arthur's Camelot.

Works Consulted

Geoffrey Ashe, *The Discovery of King Arthur*. New York: Anchor Press, 1985. One of the foremost Arthurian scholars and historians discusses the fact and fiction of King Arthur.

Albert C. Baugh, *A Literary History of England*. New York: Meredith, 1967. In this seminal work, Baugh offers insight into the literary movements involved in the compilation of the Arthurian saga.

Larry D. Benson, *Malory's Morte Darthur*. Cambridge, MA: Harvard University Press, 1976. Benson looks at the life and work of Sir Thomas Malory.

Michael J. Curley, *Geoffrey of Monmouth*. New York: Twayne, 1994. An in-depth study into the life and work of Geoffrey of Monmouth.

David Day, *The Quest for King Arthur*. London: Griffin House, 1995. Popular writer David Day draws out an accessible overview of the myths and realities of Arthur and his knights.

Christopher Dean, *Arthur of England*. Toronto: University of Toronto Press, 1987. A critical exploration of the Arthurian legend.

Henri De Briel and Manuel Herrmann, *King Arthur's Knights and the Myths of the Round Table*. Paris: Librairie C. Klincksiek, 1972. An in-depth look into the historical variations of the tales of the knights of King Arthur.

Norma Lorre Goodrich, *King Arthur*. New York and Toronto: Franklin Watts, 1986. An exemplary theoretical work that proposes new takes on an age-old legend.

Jack Lindsay, *Arthur and His Times*. London: Frederick Muller, 1958. A look at the life and times of medieval Britain and its legendary king.

Donald Maddox, *The Arthurian Romances of Chrétien de Troyes*. Cambridge, England: Cambridge University Press, 1991. An in-depth analysis of the motivations, influences, and writings of this most famous of French romantics.

Sir Thomas Malory, *Le Morte D'Arthur*. Vol. 1. London: J. M. Dent & Sons, 1906. The first volume of the original Caxton edition of Malory's famous work.

———, *Le Morte D'Arthur*. Vol. 2. London: J. M. Dent & Sons, 1906. The second volume of the original Caxton edition of Malory's famous work.

Index

Picture Credits

About the Author

Michael J. Wyly received his master of fine arts in creative writing from California State University, Long Beach. Until recently he was an instructor of English literature and language at both California State University, Long Beach, and California State University, Dominguez Hills. He has also functioned as a fiction and poetry editor for several small-press publications. Wyly currently lives and writes in Paris, France.